W9-BSW-383

·SODA·JERK·

A Richard Jackson Book

·SODA·JERK·

Poems by Cynthia Rylant
Paintings by Peter Catalanotto

ORCHARD BOOKS · NEW YORK

Text copyright © 1990 by Cynthia Rylant
Illustrations copyright © 1990 by Peter Catalanotto
All rights reserved. No part of this book may be reproduced or
transmitted in any form or by any means, electronic or
mechanical, including photocopying, recording or by any
information storage or retrieval system, without permission in
writing from the Publisher.

Orchard Books, A division of Franklin Watts, Inc.
387 Park Avenue South, New York, NY 10016

Manufactured in the United States of America. Printed by
General Offset Company, Inc. Bound by Horowitz/Rae.
The text of this book is set in 11 pt. ITC Clearface Bold.
The illustrations are watercolor painting reproduced in full
color. Book design by Mina Greenstein.
10 9 8 7 6 5 4 3 2 1

Library of Congress Cataloging-in-Publication Data
Rylant, Cynthia. Soda Jerk / by Cynthia Rylant ; illustrated by
Peter Catalanotto.   p.   cm. "A Richard Jackson book"—
Summary: A series of poems spoken by a young soda jerk in a
small town as he observes the people and places around him.
ISBN 0-531-05864-6.   ISBN 0-531-08464-7 (lib. bdg.)
1. Children's poetry, American.   [1. City and town life—
Poetry.   2. American poetry.]   I. Catalanotto, Peter,
ill.   II. Title. PS3568.Y5S64   1990   811'.54—dc20
89-35654   CIP   AC

FOR DAV PILKEY,
in friendship and admiration
C.R.

Contents

Maywell's Drugstore
has got the smell of women to it,
and for that reason
I almost didn't apply.
They needed a soda jerk
and I needed a job,
and in Cheston, Virginia
you've got to take what comes.
So I am here
frying cheeseburgers
and squirting the cream
and watching.
Everybody comes into Maywell's
at least once.
They go out the door taking
some of that woman-smell with them,
and they leave behind
some secret
with the jerk.
Tips are okay.
But the secrets are better.

Maywell's has been open
Sunday afternoons
for going on thirteen years
and the church people are still squawking.
But that doesn't stop them
coming in here after services
with their howling youngsters,
looking for strawberry cones to
jam
into their gaping little mouths.
I like working Sundays
because it gives me opportunity
to witness the Great American Family,
and I must say
such a thing
is a puzzle to me,
because everybody is talking
like they never met before,
husbands to wives,
kids to fathers,
mothers to kids,
and you wonder how long it's been
since they've seen each other
and whether they've changed much
since last they spoke
and will they find ways
not to see each other
for a long time again
till next Sunday.

When my grandaddy died
they weren't sure what to do
with his false teeth and his
one glass eye
and it is this
I sometimes think about
when there's a hot dog left over
at the end of the day
that nobody ate.
My grandaddy's glass eye
would confuse you,
because you weren't sure
which side of his nose
to look to
since
it wasn't real clear
which eye worked and which didn't.
I used to wonder
how he felt
having that marble stuck in his socket
like a stuffed moose.
And did he worry it might
pop out backwards into the gray meat
of his brain?
Or maybe fall into his
spaghetti
when he was out with Grandmama
at some nice Italian restaurant?
They finally buried
his eye and his teeth

out in the woods
behind the house.
I have thought about that a lot,
and just as I don't like
throwing out
a perfectly good hot dog
at closing time,
I hate to think there's
some other old man
who might could use
a good glass eye
or some teeth
and having to do without
just because Grandmama
didn't want to be
disrespectful.

I have got these
skinny-smooth white arms
with little brown moles
for decoration,
and it is these ugly things
I see
every time I put a
chocolate sundae
or a toasted cheese
in front of somebody.
I have been wanting man-arms
since I was ten,
and every time I go to a movie
I am looking at the arms in it,
so I miss everything important
that's going on
because I am silently
counting all the hairs
I do not have.
It's Tom Selleck
who's got the best arms
I can see,
and every night
I go to bed praying
I'll be him when I wake up
and the little hairs
from my big man-arms
will start showing up
on top of the whipped cream
or floating in somebody's coffee cup,
and pretty soon
Mr. Maywell will have to fire me
because
there's just no contending
with a soda jerk who's got
arms like these,
and the next stop for me
I guess
will be the marines.

It's just me and my dad
because
Mom got married again and
I didn't want to live
with her and her new husband.
Not that he's a bad guy,
but he's always after me
to do something with him
like fish
or bowl
or watch a game on Sunday,
and truth is when he does it
I feel like I used to
when one of those
circus clowns came after me
in a parade.
I'd be standing on the sidewalk,
about five years old,
and suddenly there'd be
this giant mouth
coming at me,
and the clown always
thought I'd laugh
but instead I'd start to bawl,
and that's how I feel
when this man starts after me
to do something with him.
My mother and him
stop in for a lemonade
now and then,

and I don't mind that
'cause they know I'm working
and they don't give me their
"Smile, Honey" routine.
My dad only said one thing
against my mother,
and that is
that she'd be better off
in California
with the other happy Munchkins,
and I guess he's right,
because lemonade
is about the only sour thing
she'll let get near her.
Which is why
I live with my dad.

You can tell the rich kids
when they come in
because they all look like
Tide commercials,
they are so clean and bright,
and you wonder why
having money
gives people clear skin,
and why it's the poor kids
who have to keep
Clearasil
in business.
Rich kids have such good mouths
they probably never
stand in front of the mirror
and practice smiling
to see if there's some way
in which to improve
on a bad thing.
Rich kids do not sweat,
or if they do
it smells like
apples.
Rich kids
are never soda jerks,
and for that reason
they will always look clean
and they will never have to
know
how much syrup
you need for a banana shake
or
how to tell
when the fries are done
or
how to get the meat
cooked in the middle.
Rich kids just know
how to sit around
making the place pretty,
which is fine
for a soda jerk
who's always loved
unpacking
the
ornaments.

Mr. Maywell is the pharmacist
as well as the owner
of the drugstore
and he is pretty all right
to work for,
except once
he tried to kiss
one of the high-school girls
working here (my information is
secondhand so you can
believe it or not),
and she threatened to tell
Mrs. Maywell plus
the minister of the church
where Mr. Maywell is a deacon
and all I know is
he's hired nothing but boys
since then,
which is lucky
for this jerk.
Still, when it's closing time
I try not to be
in the back room with him
because stories stick with you,
like it or not,
and until I grow me some
muscles and some whiskers,
I'm not hanging out
with any drugstore deacons I know.

It's the hippies who puzzle me.
They've got a little college
over in the next town
and sometimes
they'll drive into Cheston.
A few of them
will come in here
and they'll be wearing those clothes,
those clothes that are long
and look like
maybe they've got on two or three
outfits at once.
Dad says there aren't any more
hippies,
but what else would you call
these people?
They smell funny, too,
like they've been sitting in
a barrel of pumpkin-pie spice,
and they'll sit around and talk
with marbles in their mouths
about everything
that doesn't have to do
with real life.
And I keep trying to picture them
when they were little,
eating bologna-and-tomato sandwiches
and watching *I Dream of Jeannie*,
and I wonder if they miss it,

if they wouldn't just like to throw on
a pair of J.C. Penney Plain Pockets
and go to a football game
and be natural
awhile.

There's this girl comes in,
she's probably around twenty,
and I like to think about her.
I get this strong feeling at home
to think about her,
so I'll run me a big bath,
and I'll lay in the tub
and my mind'll wander.
I dream that
we've been out on a few dates
and I haven't touched even her hand.
Then on, say, date number four or five,
we're in some elevator
in some building
and we're the only ones
and before we've reached our floor,
she lets go and hits the
STOP
button.
I look at her
and she's got this serious face
then she lets go again and hits the
LIGHT
button
and there we are in the dark.
She backs me up
against the elevator wall
and she pushes up against me
and starts kissing me
like she's starving for it,

and we stay that way
a good hour or more.
Which is about how long
my bath goes,
since I like to take
a nice long time
with all this making out.
I watch for her to come
into Maywell's,
which she does often, as
she works in some office in town,
and she'll sit down and order
an egg-salad sandwich,
and every time
I am green and sick
as a dog
but I smile
and say "Sure thing!"
and act like I've got me
a girlfriend anyway.
It sure helps the time pass.

You probably will not believe this,
but one guy who graduated
from the high school
about twelve, thirteen years ago
became a rock star,
and now he's on MTV
singing about the good old days
in Cheston
when he was wearing nothing but
jeans and white T-shirts
and drinking beer out at the reservoir,
and people don't know how to act
about all this.
You'll hear them
talking about him
at the counter,
and they'll try to talk
like he's still just one of them,
like he's just working at the
hardware or something,
but you'll notice
they don't have much
breath
when the subject is him,
even though they've got plenty breath
when the subject is
Mr. Bissler liquidating
the furniture store.

And you realize then
why the Nazarenes
made such short work of Jesus.

Living in Cheston
is like living in a dream
somebody else is having.
There are days I'm standing
at Maywell's window
and the town freezes up
like stone
for me
and I'm seeing all of us
like it's forever.
Like it's never going to be
any other way
but me being a jerk
and Mr. Jacobs selling paint
and Mr. Brinzer selling chicken legs
and Mrs. Elizabeth Clark
selling little painted bunnies
to hold your messages
to the refrigerator.
There is always
the McCrorys'
and always the Jiffy-Lube
and forever the Spin-More records.
I am thinking
there is nothing for God
but Cheston, Virginia,
and no one to create
but us,

and some way we are
knowing everything we have to
and doing
everything we need to
and there's nothing else,
there's nothing more,
but me and this frozen town
that somebody's been dreaming
into life.

Dad
will stop by for a
pack of cigarettes now and then
but he never orders anything
from the fountain.
Dad owns the office-supply store
in town
and it seems like his whole life
is written up in those
little books they use,
all those red and black lines
telling
how much you ordered
and
how much you spent
and
how much you owe.
Dad must not have wanted
an office-supply store
when he was a boy
and still dreaming.
He must have wanted
to be an astronaut,
or president,
or maybe fire chief.
He must look around him
some days
at all the number-two pencils
and white bond paper
and masking tape
and carbon sheets
and wonder
how he got there.

I don't think he's much pleased
with me being
a soda jerk
either,
which is probably why
he never has a cup of coffee here
though he'll walk right over
to the Dairy Queen for one
even when it's five blocks
further north.
I think my dad
gets scared when he sees me here,
and figures
he's not done much of anything
in his life
except sell ballpoints in bulk
and father a jerk
who will never be an astronaut
or president—
and the only fire the jerk'll put out
will be
from too much fat.

My friends are always asking me whether
I sell
"sexual aids" at the drugstore
and I cannot believe how stupid
they are—
like maybe I'm just supposed to
slip a little package next to somebody's
coffee cup
with his non-dairy creamer?
But I think about it, the stuff
over there where Mr. Maywell is,
and I try to keep an eye
on who's buying what.
Either people are very slick
or I am very slow,
because I haven't yet
seen one person buy
any one of those
sexual aids,
and I am wondering
whether everybody's
driving out of town
to buy them
or else Cheston is going to see
its own little baby boom shortly.
I know
there's not a chance in a million
that I'll be needing that sort of merchandise
any time soon,
but it has occurred to me
that if I did,

I'd already be familiar
with the year, make, and model
of every piece of paraphernalia
on those shelves,
I've been looking that direction
for so long.
Of all the millions of subjects
one could be expert in,
I can't believe
it is this
I've ended up with.

Doug Oaksberry tried to kill himself
when his girlfriend dumped him
in eleventh grade.
I hear he used to talk about it
in American history.
Talked about tying that gun up
inside his car
so its barrel pointed
to his head.
Talked about it like he was
discussing good potato salad.
"I pulled the trigger,"
he'd say,
"and the blame thing missed me."
Took off part of his shoulder instead,
and he would unbutton
the top buttons of his shirt
and pull it over to the side
to give you a look
at the red scars
and skin grafts.
He'd laugh.
His old man
is funeral director in town,
which makes sense to me
though I can't
explain it.

Doug comes in
for a large RC Cola
now and then
but he's
real quiet in here.

I have been wanting to be
an actor,
but there is no way
I'll tell anybody
because around here
that's like saying you
want to be a hairdresser,
if you catch my drift,
and I'm taking no chances
in Cheston.
But I want to be an actor,
and I want to be one like
Peter O'Toole.
One of those long-looking actors
with not much chest
but those kind of eyes
that make your mouth turn up or down
and those kind of hands
like willow branches.
I practice in my room sometimes.
I set up scenes in my head
and then I whisper
them through.
I am Cyrano de Bergerac.
I am Captain Queeg.
I am the Elephant Man.
My face changes
a thousand ways
and my body becomes like sculpture,

and sometimes
in the middle of it all
I am seized with the terror
that I will stay
in Cheston, Virginia
for the rest of my life.

The old ladies love to come in
and ask Mr. Maywell
what he recommends
when they've got an itch here
or a cramp there
or they're just feeling
a little light-headed.
These old ladies
who've been somebody's mom
for so long,
they have come begging
for a person to take an interest.
Been so long since
somebody brought them
a cup of warm milk
in the middle of the night.
Their slug-husbands
never had it in them
to rub some Ben-Gay onto
anybody's shoulders
but their own,
and the grown children
are at the front door
first thing
when one of the grandkids is sick.

Old ladies needing a mom,
and poor Mr. Maywell
filling in best he can
though you know
they'd really love a hand on them—
anywhere, anywhere to be
touched—
when they're caught up
in the aches
nobody'll
allow.

When the sheriff and his deputies
come into Maywell's for their coffee,
you know that these guys,
when they got their new uniforms,
must have put them on first thing.
Must have taken that
shirt with its sewn-on badges
out of the plastic
first thing,
home alone in the bedroom,
must have buttoned it up bit by bit
and stood there looking a long time
in the mirror.
You know these guys
must have squeezed through
twelfth-grade English with a D—
because their girlfriends
cheated for them
and you know
they must dream
about
Ford Broncos
every night.
You know that for these guys
every dream
has come true
when they suit up
and get behind the wheel
of a car
with a big red siren on top.

Every day for these guys
is cowboys and Indians
and they never expected
to get paid for it.
They thought they'd be
working in the mill
or the mine
or building the new interstate.
They never dreamed
it would be recess
every day
and they'd get to play cops
every day
and they'd get to
order up black coffee
every day,
standing near enough the register
to see their reflections
in the mirror that's back of it.
These little boys sure
got what they wanted
from Santa.

If Mr. Kline ever died
I don't know what Cheston would do
because he's the only reason
we all stay here.
You walk in his market
and your shoulders let go,
and even if you only came
for a chocolate milk,
you'll turn to your right
and you'll walk past
the produce
and on by the freezer
and on past the pop
back to the meat counter
and around,
because Kline's
is like that.
It's like some primitive
Indian path
you've got to walk
because the Cherokee blood in you
is burning.
You will find your way
on over to the cooler—
which is right by the front door—
and you will pay the girls
at the register,
the girls who tape
pictures of Mel Gibson and Don Johnson
up the wooden pole beside them.

And you will pay them
pretty slow,
it is feeling so good to be there,
and Mr. Kline is moving
up from the back
and you want to
say hello to him, too,
because it's
part of that path
and you won't feel finished
if you don't.
And when you push open the door
and you're on Main Street again,
you know why it is
living in Cheston hasn't
killed you yet.

Thanksgiving
is when you'll see
dead deer strapped
to the cars,
and I tell you,
it's tough being a guy
in a place where
a deer corpse
is cause for joy among men
and it is your business
to serve up coffee
to the mighty hunters
for whom a clean shot
is a lucky shot
and who never mention
the gut shots
they let fly
and the deer
they lost
because they were too drunk
and too many inches from the heart,
so their animal
ran off
even though it was spilling its guts
in the true sense
of the word.
I hate
Thanksgiving weekend
in Maywell's
like I hate
the dog pound
and the bomb
and the black lung
and the bloated belly
and apartheid.
Dead deer tied to hoods
shake me
into an old man's rage,
and it is all I can do
to pour that coffee
for the scum who
any other weekend
I'd be real happy
to oblige.

I play guitar pretty good,
and one night
I went to this party
at Sue Sawyer's house
and I'm standing around
being the usual
beanpole jerk that I am
when I see a guitar behind a chair.
So I pull it out
and it's way out of tune
but I get it as tuned
as anyone can
and I start playing.
I'm playing some Villa-Lobos
and some Kottke
and some Albinez,
and next thing I know
I've got four or five
girls sitting there with moon eyes,
and I'm feeling like
I am the most beautiful man
in the world.
My teeth are getting straight,
my skin is clearing up,
my jaw is squaring,
and my shoulders spread like wings.
I sit there beautiful
all night long,
playing,
and the moon girls
flutter against me now and then

the way girls can do
that sends your blood
rushing to the right places.
Then wouldn't you know,
the next day I'm back at Maywell's
and sure enough they all trickle in
sometime during the day
and they seem kind of confused,
kind of like they took a wrong turn,
and there are
no moons
and no flutters,
and the jerk is a pumpkin
they could have sworn
was something else the night before.
I wipe the crumbs
off the counter and I understand
like I never did till now
why Cinderella
ran so hard
and so fast
when the clock struck twelve.

There's these three jocks
who like to come in
Friday nights,
and it's like they are doing
this *skit*
about three jocks
who like to come in
Friday nights.
First:
They're all numbered.
Jocks never put on a stitch
of anything
unless it's numbered.
Second:
Their necks collect up
all the fat
in their bodies
and hold it there like
oil kegs,
so their heads kind of swivel
on these big round chunks.
Third:
They walk with their arms sticking
out some five inches
from their bodies
like they're waiting for their
deodorant to dry,
and while I am watching
all of this I am
asking them in my head:
"Are you *kidding me*?"
Granted
they will be the ones
to take the Homecoming Court
to the dance,
and they will be the ones
to get the color photos
in the yearbook,
and they will be the ones
people'll talk about
over the gas pumps
at the Amoco.
But these jocks
are dead people.
These jocks have been dead
ever since some guy
shoved a ball into their hands
as they were climbing
out of the sandbox
and just about to have
an original thought.
But it never came,
it never had a chance to come,
therefore
they are the walking
brain-dead.
And I know
they are *not* kidding
because it takes
a personality
to kid,
and so far
all that these guys
have taken
is a number.

Sandy Jane Meador
is a popular girl
and when she comes in
she is very nice
and she smiles a lot
and she never lets there be

      a hole

in the conversation;
she never lets there be
one of those
a^{w}k^{w}a^{r}d m^{o}m^{e}n^{t}s
in life. . . .

And you are very nice
and you smile a lot
and you fill up
all the conversation holes
as fast as she does,
so Sandy Jane
will leave
feeling good about
how it all went
and thinking
how nice you are
and believing
how nice she is,
and you are so tired
from all that work

keeping the popular girl
popular.
And typical of the jerk you are,
you hope she liked you.

Pansies
are something I just love,
and who'd ever guess it?
I have sat and stared
at a bed of pansies
for hours on end
and wondered
how God
came up with such a thing.
I have this fantasy:
It is that when I die
(and this is sick
I admit),
when I die
and am in the ground
pansies will start
growing out of me.
First a couple
sprout through my eyeballs,
and then a couple more
poke out my nostrils,
and they are coming
from near every open place
of my dead body.
They push off the lid
of my coffin
and up they rise through the earth
until
the mound of my grave

is covered with
pansy faces,
and every so often
someone
comes along
and stares at them
for hours on end.
Every other boy I know
wants to be
a major-league player
or a front lineman
or something,
and I am the only
boy I know
who wants to be
a pansy bed,
which, I admit,
troubles me no end.

When Crystal Davis and her mother
stop by,
the mother acts thirteen
and Crystal acts forty
and you begin to wonder
watching them
why they get it mixed up
all the time,
if God didn't make some mistake,
wasn't paying attention
and put the Mom tag on the wrong angel
before He sent them
on down,
and now they can't do any better.
You have to feel sorry for a girl
whose mother makes eyes
at a beanpole soda jerk
who tends to get spit
coming out the corners of his mouth
when he talks.
You also have to wonder
whether Crystal
will still be around
when her mother finally grows up
just long enough
to notice
the old woman she's been raising.

Christmastime in Maywell's
is real pretty.
Mr. Maywell likes that
fat silver tinsel,
and he'll spend practically
all of a Sunday night
looping it across every square inch
of ceiling.
Then he'll hang
white plastic bells from the loops
and the store looks
like Disney World must.
At Christmas
people want hot chocolate
nine times out of ten,
and I am happy to serve it up.
I feel like I'm important
to them that way,
and it is a joy to be a jerk.
What I would really like
would be to stay open
all of Christmas Eve—
call it crazy I don't care—
and see what the night's like,
'cause I've been sleeping through
every one,
and I've got this idea
that people who work
on Christmas Eve

have got it better
than the rest of us,
provided they're connected
with the outside somehow.
I've got this idea that
I'd believe in flying reindeer again
if I worked at the fountain
through Christmas Eve.
There'd be something in the night
to prove it,
though I can't say what,
and come morning
I'd be like a tired old elf
and just soaked to the bone
in mystery.
But Mr. Maywell locks up at five,
and all that tinsel
just hangs.

There are some guys in town
with one of those car horns
that plays "Dixie,"
and every now and then
they'll cruise by the store,
wishing to be in the
land of cotton.
Most people don't like
the horn—
they'll roll their eyes up
when the car goes past—
but none of them seems stunned like me.
I hear it
and I want to run into the attic
with Anne Frank
or into the cellar
with Harriet Tubman,
and I feel like
this is a dangerous world
I'm in
and I'd better
stock up on the bottled water
just in case.
Just in case everybody
starts wanting
one of those horns.

Some mornings
I get up real early before work
and head on up
to the lake.
The slam of the car door
echoes out on the water,
and then
it's like something starts
settling down inside me.
It's settling down into the
open spaces between
my skin and my bones
as I look at that lake
all covered in fog
and gray like rabbit skin.
Sometimes a heron comes
in for a landing,
and it's just me and him,
and all of a sudden
I feel like a heron.
I stand there
and I am feeling like it's me
floating out on that water.
It's me
picking through those reeds.
It's me flapping my wings and
it's my feet
hanging down uninterested
while the rest of my body works
to fly up off that lake.

Then the heron is gone,
and the jerk is back,
chewing on the styrofoam cup in his hand and
wishing for things
he can't even put a name to.
Quarter to eight
I get back in the car,
and eight on the dot
I am walking into Maywell's.
I am there.
Crossing the floor
with heron feet,
pouring the coffee
with heron hands.
Working the day like
I'm flying.

My good friend Bob and me,
we talk about
what we'll do after graduation,
and we talk like
we've got all the choices
in the world,
but who are we kidding?
Bob's been flunking math
since he was eight,
and though he's a great one
for zoning in on things—
like he knew right off
George Griffith was going to
drop out of school
as soon as he saw him
fumble that football—
what good is that to a guy?
Sure won't buy him no
trips to Myrtle Beach.
They keep telling us
we can be anything we want.
We'll sit in my bedroom
and listen to those stars
on MTV
tell us we can make
all our dreams come true.
And we're digging into
the bag of Doritos
and looking at the TV screen
like it's men on the moon,

like we're watching
some guy in a spacesuit
telling us we can just come on up
anytime.
What Bob and me want
isn't all that much,
but it's too much,
and we're not crazy enough
to think we'll ever get it.
Bob wants to be an assistant
to a sculptor.
He saw some thing on TV
about this crazy guy
who lives in the desert
and makes these gigantic
weird shapes and gets more famous
with every one,
and Bob wants to tote
the guy's water buckets
or run for his chisels
or some such thing.
And then there's me
thinking I'm going to replace
Dustin Hoffman once
he kicks under.
Truth is, Cheston is Cheston.
And we've never learned a thing
about dreams here,
much less making them come true.
They started on us early.
They made us put every square peg
into every square hole

starting in kindergarten,
and maybe the names changed
but it has stayed square pegs
and square holes
every day since.
We busted our butts
trying to circle the right
multiple choice,
and we watched year after year
while the ones who got it—
the ones just made for a world
of square pegs and square holes—
carried off little medals
the first of June
for all the workbooks
they held sacred
and all the gold stars
that proved they were
doing things right.
Bob and me,
we could sit for hours and talk
about how trees look like
they're in certain kinds of moods,
but we'd still go in
and screw up the
language-arts quiz
because we never really gave
a flying fudrucker
whether little Bobby
saw a fountain or a farmer
when his daddy pulled the wagon
into town.

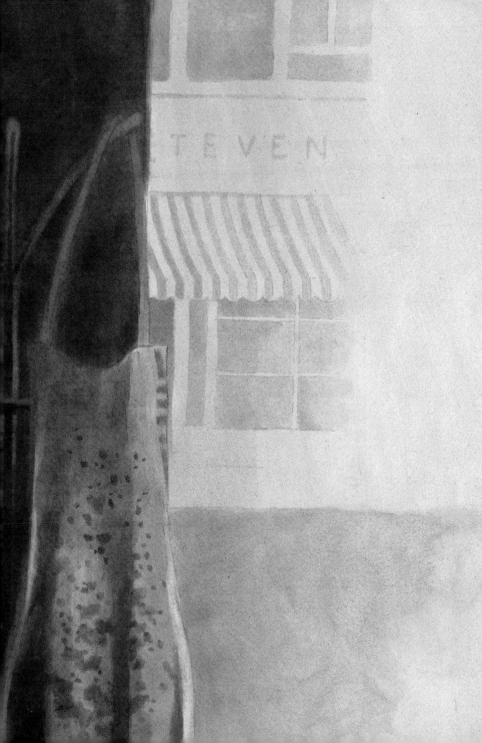

Screw little Bobby.
I've been smelling like
vanilla ice cream and ladies' perfume
nearly a year now
and I've seen plenty in Maywell's,
but I haven't seen anything that'll tell me
why some people get
what they want
and some people don't.
There's one thing though:
every day in Cheston
might be the same
as every other,
but if you're a jerk who's watching it,
who never gives up too much to it,
then even if you don't get
what you want,
at least you never slept through the
whole show.
At least you kept your ears open,
and you heard more
than just the words.
You saw more
than just the actors.
You believed in
the closing credits.

And Mr. Maywell thinks
I've just been making sodas.

Also by Cynthia Rylant

PICTURE BOOKS
Mr. Griggs' Work
All I See
Birthday Presents
Night in the Country
The Relatives Came
This Year's Garden
Miss Maggie
When I Was Young in the Mountains

"THE HENRY AND MUDGE BOOKS"

STORIES
Children of Christmas
Every Living Thing

POETRY
Waiting to Waltz: A Childhood

NOVELS
A Kindness
A Fine White Dust
A Blue-Eyed Daisy

AUTOBIOGRAPHY
But I'll Be Back Again